SHANNON NOSLEY

VIDEO BLOGGING

The Essential Guide On How You Can VLOG Your Way to Millions, Discover the Ways on How You Can Profit From Your Own Video Blogs

Descrierea CIP a Bibliotecii Naționale a României
SHANNON NOSLEY
   VIDEO BLOGGING. The Essential Guide On How You Can VLOG Your Way to Millions, Discover the Ways on How You Can Profit From Your Own Video Blogs / Shannon Nosley. – Bucharest: Editura My Ebook, 2020
   ISBN

SHANNON NOSLEY

VIDEO BLOGGING

**The Essential Guide On How You Can VLOG Your Way
to Millions, Discover the Ways on How You Can Profit
From Your Own Video Blogs**

My Ebook Publishing House
Bucharest, 2020

CONTENTS

CONTENTS

CHAPTER 1

WHAT IS VIDEO BLOGGING

Video blogging has grown in popularity over the past few years and even though many have used video blogs to create a fortune there are quite a few people who have never heard of Internet blogging. Video blogging is a close cousin of traditional blogging, the primary difference between the two is that video is used to communicate with visitors in place of text. Many Internet entrepreneurs have created their own highly successful video blogs (also known as vlogs) which are used to communicate with subscribers, potential clients, and the rest of the World Wide Web. Video blogs let visitors interact with their favorite website owners by rating video post or even creating video comments.

Blogging vs. Vlogging

Setting up a video blog site is not that much different from setting up a traditional blog. There are many websites that allow users to upload or share their videos absolutely free of charge. These video sites let users express themselves and their opinions with few restrictions. Creating the videos themselves is also relatively easy and does not require a lot of filming experience or expensive equipment.

Are Video Blogs Popular?

To date there are thousands of video blogs online today with hundreds of thousands of readers and millions of video clips. Some aspiring actors and comedians have even started scripting their own video blogs. These days there are even casting calls for actors to star in Internet based shows that are broadcasts on video blogs. Quite a few Internet celebrities owe their fame to their own video blogs which have been seen and adored by millions. A few video bloggers have even become celebrities with millions of online fans. A few of these web celebs are:

- Jessica Rose also known as LonelyGirl 15
- Amanda Congdon of Rocketboom
- Perez Hilton
- Seth Gordon
- Jeff Jarvis of BuzzMachine

- Hosea Frank also known as ZeFrank
- Harry Knowles of Aintitcoo

Well known corporations have also started operating video blogs that are dedicated to providing individuals with visual content. In addition to businesses operating video blogs high ranking CEOs have also started their own video blogs. These vlogs give consumers and investors a chance to get to know more about powerful companies and the people who are running them. A few well known personalities and musicians like Oprah Winfrey and even the Queen of England have started their own video blogs.

Many people are shocked by the idea of famous media stars and royalty taking the time to establish video blogs but the reality is video blogs are the future of online marketing.

Viral videos are taking over the Internet and marketing firms are becoming aware of it. Video blogs have helped people from all backgrounds gain Internet popularity and earn money online.

This ebook is designed to teach novice bloggers how to successfully start their own popular, extremely profitable, video blog. The book will tell you how to set up your own video blog using popular blogging platforms. It will also tell you many ways to profit from your new video blog and how to effectively market it. This ebook provides you with detailed information and many resources that will save you a great deal of time and energy that would have been spent in research along with time and error.

Chapter Recap

- Video blogs, also known as vlogs, combine video with blogging.
- Creating videos for vlogs does not require expensive equipment or extensive technical knowledge.
- Many video bloggers have acquired Internet fame and fortune thanks to their popular video blog posts.
- Famous people, even royalty, and well known corporations have established their own video blogs.

CHAPTER 2

WHY YOU SHOULD START A VIDEO BLOG

Now that you know what a video blog it is you might be wondering why you should start one. You might be thinking a traditional blog might be perfect for your needs. If you already have an established blog you might be wondering whether or not you should spend time adding video posts to your existing site. The truth is that there are many benefits associated with running your own video blog site that simply cannot be found elsewhere. For starters a video lets you, the website owner, communicate and reach visitors more effectively than words. There are some things that simply cannot be expressed well in writing.

Video blogs are also a great way to truly express opinions and feels on certain hot topics or controversial issues. Your website is uncensored and gives you an opportunity to share your opinions freely but sometimes writing will not truly illustrate your feelings to readers. A video will let visitors hear your tones be they joking or angry. Video blogs also let visitors see facial expressions, gestures, or even conversations if the blog features more than one person.

In the event that you website has been set up for personal use a video blog will give you a chance to share important moments with friends and family across the globe. The posts can feature video showing weddings, parties, and other events in your life. A video blog is also a way for new families to show the growth and activity of their young children such as birthdays, first steps, and more.

Video blogs are also perfect for capturing the attention of a sometimes fickle audience. Many visitors get bored by posts, especially long posts with a lot of technical detail.

Even if the information is something that will be useful to them readers get frustrated when they simply cannot visualize what they are reading. A video will help prevent your readers from growing frustrated and will also help your website capitalize on the growing popularity of video blogs.

Posting videos on your website will also let visitors know that you, the website owner, are serious about spreading your message. More importantly, posting videos of yourself explaining a product or service will let your visitors know that you are REAL and your website is legitimate. With the Internet being filled with scam artists and pretenders promoting get rich quick schemes videos will help give you a level of creditability that many website owners simply do not have. This is especially useful if you are promoting an affiliate program, products, or services.

Chapter Recap

- Video blogs let owners express themselves to visitors using tone and facial expression.
- Personal vlogs can be used to share important events in your life and the lives of your family members.
- Site visitors often prefer watching short videos than reading long text posts.
- Video blog posts featuring the site owner gives the website more credibility.

CHAPTER 3

HOW TO START A VIDEO BLOG

You now know the, what and why of video blogging, now it is time to focus on how you should go about starting your own profitable video blog. Starting a video blog is not as complicated as some believe. There are many software developers who have created free software programs that make it easy for video bloggers to post videos to their blog sites. In fact, the primary difference between video blogging and traditional blogging is the way content is presented to visitors. This difference is what makes starting a video blog a little bit more difficult than establishing a traditional blog since website owners need equipment to create videos for their blogs.

Choose a Platform

With that in mind the first thing that you should do when getting ready to set up your video blog is to pick out a blogging format. Some people prefer to depend entirely on video blogging communities but it is best to invest in your own, independent, website. A great platform for you to use is Wordpress.

I have used Wordpress successfully for video blogs and traditional blogs. It is extremely easy to install and update plus there are many websites that are designed to show new users how to use it. One of the primary reasons that I recommend Wordpress is that the platform has a feature which allows you to automatically post scheduled posts. This means that you create and upload many video blog posts and set the date and time for them to post to a day far in the future. Doing this will let you continue adding posts to your blog even if you are not around.

If you want to test drive Wordpress for free visit Wordpress.com and sign up for a free account that you can use to get used to the platform and blogging in general.

Setting up a Web Address

From there, pick out a domain name that will catch the attention of visitors and relates to the primary topics you will be discussing in your posts or video performances. One word domain names are the best but if you cannot register one word then choose two.

Avoid hyphens if possible and always choose a phrase or name that visitors will remember without confusion.

Finding a Web Hosting Company

Next, find a web hosting company that will let you register your domain name, host your website, and install Wordpress with little or no knowledge. There are two web hosting companies that provide these services and have great customer service. These two companies are Hostgator and Dreamhost.

Setting up Shop

When you have successfully signed up for a domain name, web hosting account, and installed Wordpress experiment with the Wordpress platform until you have grown comfortable with the content management platform and blogging in general. This is extremely important if you have no blogging experience. Also, find a good theme that will impress visitors and make your website look more professional. Some free Wordpress theme sites are:

- Wpthemesfree.com
- Freewpthemes.net
- Fresheezy.com

16

- WpSkins.org

You can also go to your favorite search engine and do a search for Wordpress Themes and you will get loads of options!

Always customize your free theme to showcase your websites domain name or a logo. If possible and your budget permits hire a Wordpress theme designer. Some freelance designers can be found that charge between $50.00 and $200.00 to create a completely customized theme for your Wordpress site. This theme creation will also sometimes include logo creation. Great places to find affordable freelance website designers are:

- Sitepoint.com
- Craigslist.org
- DeviantArt.com

Getting the Equipment

When searching for equipment to create the videos for your video blog it is not necessary to focus on getting the most expensive equipment on the market. Instead focus on equipment that will help you produce a viewable video blog that will be enjoyed by viewers. There are a few basic pieces of equipment that you will need to start your blog and these pieces of equipment are:

- A reliable computer with Internet access with a lot of storage capacity.
- Easy to use/understand video editing software.
- Camera or Camcorder for video and picture capture.
- 66" + tripod for mounting your camera/camcorder.
- A good microphone for additional audio capture.

Most individuals hoping to start a video blog already own a reliable computer, have Internet access, and can free storage space if an adequate amount of storage space is not available. In the event that you own a computer which only has a small amount of storage space there are ways to add an additional hard drive onto your computer giving you the storage space necessary to manage your video files. Many computers also come with video editing software, usually Windows Movie Maker or iMovie.

If you do not have video editing software on your computer here is a short list of popular video programs:

- Final Cut Pro (Mac/Paid)
- Windows Movie Maker (PC/Paid)

- iMovie (Mac/Paid)

- Avid Media Composer (PC/Paid)

- Roxio Video Wave (PC/Paid)

- Open Movie Editor (Linux/Free)

- Mewa Film (PC/Free)

There are many new video editing software programs released daily and many come with a free trial. To find free video editing software or to get reviews on paid video editing software visit CNET.com and Download.com. Both sites provide user reviews of the latest video editing programs. Some digital cameras and digital camcorders even come with video editing software.

You will also need to acquire software that can be used to convert your videos into a variety of file types. Many videos you create will originally be in MPEG4 format and not all sites accept this format. Some websites that you will eventually want to upload your videos to will automatically convert your file but this can be a slow process. It is best to convert them yourself using one of the following programs:

- AVS Video Converter

- Roxio Easy Media Creator

- Gear Video
- Any Video Converter
- CinemaForge
- Windows Media Encoder
- MPEG Streamclip
- Movavi

Owning a video editing program is an extremely important part of running a video blog. While many vlog owners simply create a video and post it on there blogs using software to edit your videos will help increase your vlogs popularity and the quality of video you are providing your viewers. This will be very important when you start vlogging for money.

A camcorder or camera that makes digital videos is also necessary to start a video blog. If you are working on a budget or do not want to invest a lot of money in a new venture you can start out using a camera phone that will take short videos. Since most camera phones only take 30 seconds worth of coverage and generally produce poor quality film you will probably have to use your editing software to sync the many short clips together and enhance the quality of the film.

Web cameras are another affordable alternative and are better to use than a camera phone. A web camera will make it easier for you to film yourself if you are running a one person show. The web camera can be mounted on a tripod giving you more control and flexibility when filming yourself and can be purchased for as little as $10.00 online and at certain retailers. They can be used to create longer video clips than a cell phone, plus they can be used for taking still photographs.

Digital cameras and camcorders are the preferred choice of many serious video bloggers. They produce higher quality videos and can be used to record extremely long clips. Quite a few video bloggers use them to create long how-to or explanatory videos that are later split up into shorter, blog friendly, clips. The downside to choosing digital cameras or camcorders is that they cost much more than web cameras and are not always as accessible as camera phones. A good digital camera can cost a minimum of $200.00 and a digital camcorder can cost at least $400.00.

There are ways to avoid spending a large amount of money for a new digital camera or camcorder. One way to save money is to borrow or buy a camera/camcorder from a friend or relative. More people than you imagine have purchased expensive cameras and camcorders only to upgrade to an even more expensive version a year or two later.

These people are usually more than willing to sell or give the old equipment to close friends or family who need them. If you do not know anyone with a used digital camera or camcorder consider purchasing one online at a discount store. When doing this always buy from a store with a return and refund policy. Also visit your local retailers that sell display or customer return cameras and camcorders. Wal-Mart and Best Buy often sell items this way for 50% or more off and buyers can benefit from an extended return policy and even additional discounts.

Microphones can be purchased at many retailers that sell software and computer equipment. They can also be purchased online for an affordable price through many different online retailers like Walmart.com Target.com and even Amazon.com. A good microphone is necessary when you are using a web camera and your computer does not have a high quality microphone built in. In other situations you might need to add audio commentary or explanations to the video clip after it has already been filmed.

Tripods are also needed for mounting digital cameras, camcorders, and even web cameras. A good tripod can be placed on nearly any surface and will allow you to record video anywhere in your house without any assistance. Wal-Mart and other retailers sell tripods in there camera and video equipment sections. The best tripods can be found in retail locations specializing in photography. Purchasing Tripods online at places like Amazon.com and even Ebay.com will help you get a great deal but should only be used when you have time to wait for the item to be shipped.

Creating a Video Post

When you have all of the equipment you need to make your video posts then you are ready to get started. Pick out a location that is interesting and clean! No one wants to see a messy room as a background. If you are more comfortable making a video using a plain background hang a sold color sheet or piece of fabric behind you since that is more interesting than a beige or white wall. Create a short video clip for your first video blog post and upload it to your computer.

Use your video editing software to make changes to your video. Enhance the quality of your video by making colors more video, increasing the focus, or even changing your color video to black and white. Add any affects that you feel would be useful such as a fade in or out and even music. Also use text affects to insert the domain name of your website and/or your logo so that if your video is shared or distributed later viewers will always know where it came from.

As soon as you are happy with your video use your editing software to compress the video into a small file size. This is necessary to ensure fast loading and easy viewing of your video. In addition to helping your visitors some websites only allow videos of a certain size to be uploaded so the smaller you compress your video the better.

Remember, compressing a video will affect its quality so only compress your video as much as needed and not more.

Uploading a Video to Your Blog

There are two easy ways that you can use to upload your videos to your video blog. The first way is to upload your video to your own channel on YouTube or a similar site that is free and easy to use. These websites will help your own site get traffic and will also let you easily embed your video onto your own vlog. This is perfect for those using free blogging platforms like Blogger.com. If you have invested in your own Wordpress blog and domain as suggested then you have the option of uploading your video the same method or upload your video to a folder in on your domain and use a video plugin to show the video on your blog. A few plugins that can be used are:

- XHTML Video Embed
- FLV Embed
- Embedded Video With Link

When you have created your video clip and posted it on your vlog you have successful created your first post! Now your video blog is up, running, and ready to be viewed it is time to start making your money.

Chapter Recap

- Create your vlog using a blogging platform such Wordpress.
- Invest in a domain name and web hosting account with one click Wordpress install such as Dreamhost.com or Hostgator.com
- Acquire a camera for creating videos, video editing software, a microphone, and a tripod for creating your video posts.

- Discounted equipment can be found at Wal-Mart and Best Buy in the form of customer returned items or previous display items.
- Edit your videos to include your domain name, special effects, and/or music.

CHAPTER 4

PROFIT FROM YOUR VIDEO BLOG

Once your video blog has been successfully set up and you are comfortable with the process of creating and posting videos to your vlog then you are ready to start making money.

One of the benefits of running a video blog for profit is that they are easy to manage and extremely popular with subscribers all over the Internet. In addition to being popular with subscribers they are very search engine friendly. Since vlogs are run on the same platform as a traditional blog they are optimized for maximum search engine performance. They also give you a chance to connect with your audience in a much more effective manner than writing ever could.

There are many ways to make money by posting videos to your blog and honestly the only limit is your imagination. The following are popular, tried and true methods that can turn your video blog into a profit making machine.

1. Ad Revenue

There are several ways for you the earn money on your video blog with the help of sponsored ads. Most people concentrate on earning money from ads based on the visitors going to the website of the sponsor. Since video blogs receive a lot of traffic, focus on earning money through pay per impression advertisement programs. These programs pay you, the vlog owner, based on the number of times their ad is displayed on a visitor's page. Pay per impression programs include:

- TribalFusion
- FastClick
- CasaleMedia
- ValueClick
- MaxOnline
- BurstMedia
- RealTechNetwork

These programs are great since they pay you for ever 1,000 times your page is loaded. They do not depend on the action of the visitor meaning you will still earn money even if your visitor doesn't click on a link, sign up for a program, or anything else.

This is a great, easy, way to benefit from the traffic that your vlog will receive. Successful vlog owners often receive $40.00 each day in ad revenue alone!

Pay per click ad campaigns are another way to earn money from your blog. These often pay more than pay per impression programs but they depend on the user clicking the advertisement or visiting an outside site. Popular pay per click programs includes:

- Google
- Yahoo Publisher Network
- Clicksor
- All Feeds
- Fast Click
- Veoda
- Bidvertiser
- Revenue Pilot

Those that have not had much luck with pay per click programs in the past might not be to eager to use these programs. It is true that it can be hard to earn a decent amount of money with click through programs but what many do not realize is that video blogs have a much higher click through rate than traditional blogs and websites. Many video blog owners have a click through rate of at least 25%.

2. Paying Video Content

There are companies that let you use their video content and will pay you each time a visitor views it by loading your website. This source of income is great for people who are not able to create a video more than once or twice a week. In order to make the most of your video blog you will need to post daily and using this source of content will let you post fresh videos each day and allow you to earn money each time someone views this video. A great source of this type of content is Voxant.com.

Voxant.com also known as TheNewsRoom.com is a fantastic way to provide your video blog visitors with content at no charge to yourself. Not only will you be receiving content free of charge, you will be paid for the privilege. Regardless of your chose niche you will be able to find video content for your video blog. Voxant.com has financial news, entertainment information, celebrity gossip, and more.

3. Distribute Your Videos for Cash

There are now websites similar to YouTube that allow video creators to upload their video blog entries and earn money each time they are viewed. Not only will this help your own vlog receive traffic, it will also help you earn money. Video bloggers have earned thousands of dollars by utilizing this method. Sites that will pay you for sharing your vlog posts are:

- MetaCafe.com
- Break.com
- Revver.com
- Flixya.com

Using these sites will help you earn money while expanding your reach and bringing traffic to your website. Plus these sites are all extremely easy to use. Once you have created your videos for your blog upload the content to these sites. As long as your content is original and entertaining you will be able to earn money each time someone views it. The sites are set up to allow visitors to embed your video onto their blogs or other sites which increase your views and income.

4. Promote Affiliate Programs/Products With Video Posts

Sign up for affiliate programs that sell products and services that you yourself utilized. Once you have become an affiliate create videos that show you using and benefiting from the service product. A picture is worth a thousand words and a video is worth a million. People like to see what they are going to buy before they buy and they certainly want to see it in action. Most of us have been encouraged to purchase items based on 30 second commercials aired on television. Think of what sort of affect a video can have on your affiliate sales.

If you are someone that has not had luck with affiliate programs in the past do not be afraid to try again. Video blogging will do wonders to increase your sales. Website visitors will be encouraged by the fact that you do not only promote the product, you also use it.

There are many companies online that offer affiliate programs to let website owners profit from encouraging others to buy various products or invest in certain services. Choose a product that you personally enjoy since that will make it easier for you to create energetic, enthusiastic, video blog posts. Pick a company selling clothing, DVDs, CDs or books that you like and become an affiliate. A few companies to consider are:

- Road Kill Tshirts
- Netflix
- BMG Music
- Bookwise

- Mia Bella Candles
- Avon
- Mary Kay
- Entertain with Ease
- Jerky Direct
- Traveling Vineyard

5. Create Membership Areas

If you have created a video blog covering a specific niche then you can profit by creating a members only area. This can be especially useful to those who are making instructional videos are videos that are designed for a certain niche audience. Reserve some especially informative video posts for your member areas.

Also advertise additional bonuses to those who become paying members to your video blog. Offer small gifts, free downloads, any bonus that would appeal to your visitors that would not cost you much money if anything. Charge a monthly or yearly membership fee that would provide additional money to your video blog. Some video blog owners charge as much as $70.00 per yearly sign up.

6. Sell Video Ad Space

Think of how much money the average company spends to create and air commercials. Most small companies cannot manage that especially small, Internet based, companies. Offer to create video testimonial/commercials promoting certain products or services.

There are many businesses that would benefit from this and you can get cash and free products by doing this! Advertise your services on sites like:

- Sitepoint.com
- Craigslist.org
- Ebay.com

When advertising your services come up with pricing guidelines and place ads offering your services in the small business sections or advertisement space for sale. Let them know that you will be creating a customized video that they will be able to use on their own site. This offer alone will get the attention of many business owners who are promoting new products are creating new advertisement campaigns.

When it comes to using these profit generating methods do not limit yourself to just one. It is entirely possible to take advantage of all of the previously mentioned guaranteed money making methods to increase the revenue of your new video blog. In addition to the methods outlined there are other things that you can do to generate income using your blog. You can create video testimonials for companies that will pay for the promotion or even sell your own products on sites like Ebay.com or Etsy.com creating videos of yourself using or even making the products you intend to sell.

Chapter Recap

- Use cost per impression ad programs to earn money whenever a viewer visits your new vlog site.
- Supplement your own video content with videos from Voxant.com to make money while entertaining your visitors.
- Get paid to let others view and distribute your video posts.
- Become an affiliate to companies with products you use and create video posts of yourself using the products.
- Sell memberships to display exclusive video content.
- Offer to create video testimonials promoting other products and services.

CHAPTER 5

PROMOTING YOUR BLOG

In order to earn the maximum amount of money possible with your new video blog you must do everything you can to market your video blog. The popularity of video blogging and search engine friendliness of blogging will give your vlog a running start but it is important that you spend some time on your own increasing your audience.

Remember, the more traffic you bring in the more money you will earn each and every day.

1. Sign up for free video communities

There are many free video communities online today that have thousands of active members. It is important that you sign up for as many communities as possible and upload fresh content to them at least once a week. This will help attract people who, once they have seen your videos, will want to view them all. Some of the best communities to participate in are:

- YouTube
- DailyMotion
- MySpace
- Google Video
- Blip.tv
- Buzznet
- Crackle
- EngagedMedia
- GoFish
- GamesVideos
- iFilm
- Hulu
- JibJab
- Kewego
- Liveleak
- MSN Soapbox
- MyVideo
- OneWorldTV
- OurMedia
- Peekvid
- Phpmotion
- Rambler Vision

- Realtime TV
- Twango
- Veoh
- Vuze

In addition to helping your vlog attract more visitors, these sites will also help your search engine ranking. By linking your website to these highly ranked video communities you will be increasing your own search engine status.

2. Sign up with Blog Networks

Always remember that your video blog is still a blog and take advantage of the traffic provided by blog directories and networks. The more you are a member of the more traffic you will receive and the better your own website will rank with search engines.

- BlogCatalog
- Blogged
- GeekySpeaky
- Blogotion
- MyBlog2U
- Webloogle

- Blog Listing
- BlogFlux
- Bloggeries
- BloggersPoint.com
- Bloghub
- BlogRankings
- BlogRater
- BlogTopSites
- Blogwise
- ExactSeek
- LSBlogs
- Top100Blogger

3. Comment Major Blogs/Vlogs

Leave comments on highly traffic, popular blogs and video blogs. Always contribute to the post to avoid being labeled as spam and include a link back to your own video blog. This will help you rank higher with the search engines and will help you get traffic when curious readers visit your blog. A few high ranking blogs to comment on are:

- Boing Boing.net
- BuzzMachine.com
- Consumerist.com
- Deadspin.com
- Defamer.com

4. Create Video Comments/Responses

Take the time to create video comments in response to other video blogs. This is a great way to get attention and traffic on website such as YouTube. A video response will often get much more attention than a text comment. You can also create video comments in response to other vlog sites and simply post links to you response in your comment on their site. This will also help you get attention and traffic.

5. Explore Social Bookmarking

Social bookmarking is a wonderful way to drive traffic to your websites and make the search engines take notice. Social bookmarks have become extremely popular with blog owners, video blog owners, and traditional website owners. Some social bookmarking sites to use are:

- BookmarkSync
- Del.icio.us
- Connotea
- Digg
- Diigo
- Furl
- GiveALink.org
- Linkwad
- My Web
- Mister Wong
- Mixx
- Newsvine
- Reddit
- Simpy
- SiteBar
- StumbleUpon

6. Use Stumble Exchange

Even though many website and video blog owners have come to understand the importance of social bookmarking they are unaware of the many sites that have sprung up to work hand in hand with social bookmarking sites. Stumbleexchange.com is one of these sites that is extremely useful. The website allows users to sign up and they stumble each others listed sites. This helps stumbleupon.com users by providing them with more traffic since the site sends the more popular websites the most traffic. Using this service will provide you with 200 to 300 unique users each day months after you stop using it.

7. Take Advantage of RSS Feed Management Services

Use RSS feed management services to help subscribers keep track of your latest video entries. Signing up for a good feed management service will help you keep track of the number of subscribers your video blog has and will help them keep track of your posts. Your users will also be able to share your feed with others.

- Feedburner
- Zookoda
- Ice Rocket
- RapidFeeds

8. Use Ping Services

Pinging services are used to notify search engines whenever you upload new content on your video blog. There are many sites to ping to and Wordpress makes it easy for video bloggers to make sure that their updates are noticed. I cannot stress how important it is to take advantage of these services. By including the following list into your Wordpress list of services to ping you will notice a substantial increase to your websites existing traffic.

Note: These sites tend to change so some links will need to be checked. This is the nature of these types of sites.

http://api.feedster.com/ping   http://api.moreover.com/RPC2

http://api.moreover.com/ping   http://api.my.yahoo.com/RPC2

http://api.my.yahoo.com/rss/ping

http://www.bitacoles.net/ping.php   http://bitacoras.net/ping

http://blogdb.jp/xmlrpc   http://www.blogdigger.com/RPC2

http://blogmatcher.com/u.php   http://www.blogoole.com/ping/

http://www.blogoon.net/ping/   http://www.blogroots.com/

http://www.blogshares.com/rpc.php

http://www.blogsnow.com/ping

http://www.blogstreet.com/xrbin/xmlrpc.cgi

http://blog.goo.ne.jp/XMLRPC   http://bulkfeeds.net/rpc

http://coreblog.org/ping/   http://www.lasermemory.com/lsrpc/

http://mod-pubsub.org/kn_apps/blogchatt

http://www.mod-pubsub.org/kn_apps/blogchatter/ping.php

http://www.newsisfree.com/xmlrpctest.php

http://ping.amagle.com/

http://ping.bitacoras.com http://ping.blo.gs/

http://ping.bloggers.jp/rpc/   http://ping.blogmura.jp/rpc/

http://ping.cocolog-nifty.com/xmlrpc

http://ping.exblog.jp/xmlrpc   http://ping.feedburner.com

http://ping.myblog.jp   http://ping.rootblog.com/rpc.php

http://ping.syndic8.com/xmlrpc.php

http://ping.weblogalot.com/rpc.php   http://ping.weblogs.se/

http://pingoat.com/goat/RPC2

http://www.popdex.com/addsite.php

http://rcs.datashed.net/RPC2/

http://rpc.blogbuzzmachine.com/RPC2

http://rpc.blogrolling.com/pinger/

http://rpc.icerocket.com:10080/   http://rpc.pingomatic.com/

http://rpc.technorati.com/rpc/ping http://rpc.weblogs.com/RPC2

http://www.snipsnap.org/RPC2

http://trackback.bakeinu.jp/bakeping.php

http://topicexchange.com/RPC2

http://www.weblogues.com/RPC   http://xping.pubsub.com/ping

http://xmlrpc.blogg.de

9. Plan Your Videos Carefully to Impress Visitors

Word of mouth is a great way to get free traffic for your new video blog. One great way to get traffic is to impress visitors with the quality and content in your videos. Plan each video before you start filming. Decide what you want the content to be meaning if you want the video to be informative, entertaining, or simply promotional.

Once you have decided what you want to make your video post about you should figure out ways to make it entertaining. Think about what your visitors want to watch. If you have a hard time imagining what your video blog visitors will want to see think about what you like to see when you are watching television or surfing the Internet for videos. Do you want to watch someone sitting in front of a computer talking woodenly in nothing but monotone? Do you want to squint at a dark blurry screen trying to figure out what images you are seen? The answer to both of these questions is no.

When you are creating your video posts always use the highest resolution settings available to get a focused image.

Also, shoot your videos in an area with a lot of lighting either natural or artificial. Last, but not least, be entertaining. Laugh, joke, and talk in a relaxed, engaging manner. Use visual aids and consider taking notes and setting them up just behind the camera to help prompt you. No viewer wants to sit through uncomfortable pauses or excessive hemming and hawing.

10. Surprise Your Visitors

Do not let your visitors get too comfortable with your video style. I cannot stress how fickle some subscribers can be. Do what you can to change your videos and make them unique or different from each other.

Change locations often especially if you usually make your videos in front of a plan back drop. Create a video outside, at a park, in a place of business that doesn't mind you making a quick video (this is one of the times that I recommend using a camera phone) and other unique places. Also try to capture video footage of anything strange or unusual as it happens around you.

Try to include guest video bloggers when possible. Many major blogs and a few minor ones boast guest bloggers and there is no reason that you cannot do the same. Try to interview someone in a field that relates to your video blog. Maybe ask a friend to create a video blog for you or with you. Doing things like that will keep your visitors attention and encourage them to check your vlog often to find out what new things are happening.

11. Promote Your Site in Your Posts

When you are creating video posts to describe a certain product, service, or even movie it is easy to focus on the information you plan to provide and forget everything else.

This is a good way to accidentally lose traffic or to help someone else benefit from your hard work. Especially if you are uploading your video posts to multiple video sharing communities. These communities allow users to post your video on multiple sites which means that you must have a way to tell all viewers where the video came from originally.

There are several ways to promote yourself the first way is to always start out your video blogs with an introduction. Say hello to your viewers and tell them your name and the domain name is your site. This is usually easy to remember and will help "brand" your video posts. If possible end your video posts by thanking the viewer for watching and mention your domain name one more time. When done right it will not sound out of place and will encourage viewers to come back to your site.

Even when you are able to mention the domain name in your video also use your editing software to insert the domain name on your video. The video editing software recommended in this ebook all make it easy to insert text in your video. Doing this will help ensure that anyone who sees the video will know where the video originally came from.

12. Update Your Blog Daily

Daily updates do more for a blogs traffic than many people realize. Think of the promotion techniques that have just been explained. Two of these include notifying subscribers about new video blog posts and notifying search engines of new blog posts. Signing up for services that will help notify people of posts is useless if you are never updating anything.

Post to your blog each and every day with a video either yours or the content of another video site that will entertain your viewers. Updating daily will constantly expose your video blog to the search engines drastically increasing your sites traffic. It will also keep your readers coming back often to check for updates.

13. Respond to Comments

Many new video bloggers and traditional bloggers never bother to respond to comments left for them. This is a serious mistake. Responding to comments lets visitors know that you are paying attention to who is coming to the site and are interested in interacting with them. This will help set you apart from the many, automated, video blogs out there that are not run by a full time person.

In addition to letting visitors know that you are willing to interact it will give them another reason to check your video blog. If they are a person that leaves a comment for you on your video blog and they believe you will answer they will have a reason to check your video blog often to see if you, or anyone else, have responded to them. When you have a few people commenting regularly consider creating a video response.

Your visitors will be extremely flattered if you take the time to create an entire video clip just to address their comments or concerned. They will also continue commenting in the hope that you respond in that fashion again.

14. Uses Articles to Promote Your Vlog

Not all places will let you upload your video posts but that doesn't mean you can't use them to promote your video blog. Write articles about the benefits of creating video blogs or even the subject of your video blogs. Include links to your own video blog as reference and watch your traffic grow. Sites to write, and submit, articles to include:

- EzineArticles.com
- ArticlesBase.com
- HubPages
- Squidoo
- Associated Content
- Triond
- Helium

These websites not only let you promote your video blog, they will also let you earn income from your articles. HubPages will let you earn affiliate income through Google Adsense, Ebay, and Amazon affiliate programs. Squidoo, Associated Content, Helium, and Triond will all provide you with income based on the amount of traffic that your article makes. If you are someone that has a hard time writing articles or if you are a person who simply does not have the time to spend writing and promoting articles consider hiring a ghostwriter or article submission service.

Chapter Recap

- Build traffic to your site to help increase your income.
- Sign up for free video sharing communities.
- Leave comments on major blogs and video blogs.
- Create video responses and comments to other videos.
- Keep site visitors entertained by changing locations and promoting guest blogs.
- Write articles to help promote your blog.
- Post to your blog daily to keep visitors and search engines interested.
- Utilize RSS feed services and ping your blogs automatically each time you post.
- Use social bookmarking sites to promote your site and help improve traffic.
- Always mention your domain name in your video posts and embed it on your video posts using editing software.

CHAPTER 6

THINGS TO REMEMBER

Knowing how to set up a video blog and create content to it is only part of owning and running a financially successful video blog. It is important that you remember the small things in order to avoid any trouble or complications later on. Doing your best to plan for all events will help you in the long run.

Read Everything

Always read over any user agreement or term of service that you are asked to sign. Especially for any service that you are using to generate income for your new video blog. Many people make the mistake of glancing over or ignoring the contracts that are asked to sign and that is always a step in the wrong direction.

Before signing up for any pay per impression or pay per click program read all parts of the user agreement and terms of service. Do the same for any affiliate programs that you will be promoting on your website. It is important that you know what forms of traffic generation and promotion are acceptable. You do not want to do anything that will be frowned upon by the company you are promoting. Many of these ad revenue and affiliate programs will freeze your accounts if they feel you have violated any of there terms.

Ask Questions

If there is anything that you do not understand, never hesitate to ask. Contact the customer service department directly and keep track of how long it takes for them to get back to you. If you are not quite sure of the answers you receive look for others that have used the program or company that you have questions about. There are many communities and forums aimed at affiliates and website owners that have members who have used the program.

Keep it Short

Do not go overboard when creating your video posts. Just because you can create a thirty minute video does not need you need to post a thirty minute video. Most Internet users are not willing to sit through a thirty minute video post. Instead keep your videos short and simple.

If possible keep your video post down to 2 minutes. This will give you enough time to quickly address whatever topic you want or give a bit of feedback. Even though many surfers do not want to spend 2 minutes reading a post they are more than willing to spend watch 2 minutes watching a post.

In the event that you have created an extremely long instructional video or are posting a video of a long event like a graduation use your video editing software to break the video up into segments. Try to keep the segments down to four minutes and give each segments titles that include something like "Part 1 of 4" to keep down confusion. Especially if you later plan to distribute the videos on websites like YouTube.

Keep it Simple

When you are editing your video keep the goal of your video in mind. Do not go overboard with effects and other special features. Remember that you are trying to present your viewers with an entertaining, viewable, video post.

During the editing process try to stick to effects that help the audio and visual aspects of the video. Bringing the picture in to focus, dubbing over audio that was recorded with a microphone, and things of that nature. Do not fall into the habit of playing loud, blaring music in the background or for an entrance and exit. Keep things plain, easy to view, and overall simple.

Remember Quality

Try your best to produce the best quality video possible. The Internet is filled with amateur video bloggers and video content producers. Do your best to stand out in the crowd. Create a video that is easy for viewers to see especially after they have been compressed.

Shoot your videos in the best quality lighting possible. Always use a well lit room or, if that is not an option, natural light. Create your video during the day and open up windows, blinds, etc. until you are sure that you have plenty of good quality light available for shooting your video. Also shoot your video using the highest resolution setting possible. Many new digital camera and camcorder owners do not know how to adjust their resolution settings and accidentally film using the lowest resolution settings creating low quality film. Read your user manual to find out how to change your resolution.

Entertain Them

Always remember to entertain your viewers. Even if the information you are presenting is by nature a bit boring or dull do what you can to liven it up. Viewers are not coming to your video blog to stare at a person sitting in front of a computer making a vapid observation before quickly fading out of view.

Interact with your invisible audience in the same manner you would if they were with you. Smile, be animated and energetic. If you do not seem to care about what you are talking about neither will anyone else. Do not be afraid to use visuals such as books, videos, or CDs that relate to the topic of your video blog post. Not only will this give you something to do with your hands, it will also help with your over all presentation.

Script It

One of the primary complaints viewers have about video blogs is the fact that the blogger will forget what they are talking about. I have already mentioned that it is hard to memorize even a four minute blog post but people always try to do it anyway. Video bloggers want to appear authentic and spontaneous but think of things this way. Some of the most popular video blogs on the Internet feature people who are using scripted or pre-rehearsed parts.

While you might not want to pre-rehearse what you are going to say you do want to at least write it down and keep notes some where handy. Try to use your computer screen as a teleprompter by scrolling text across it or post notes of what you want to discuss behind your camera. Do what you can to help jog your memory and prevent your video post from being filled with "Umm.. Like... Uhh..". You might feel like you are cheating viewers out of an authentic video blog but trust me, they will enjoy watching your scripted video journal better than an improved one.

Don't Forget Your Fans

Once you have gone through all of the hard work of building your video blog, establishing traffic, and earning a steady income do not forget your audience. It is easy for video bloggers to get lax with blog posting after they have earned a good deal of money or notice that money is coming in steadily from their monotonies video blog. The problem with thinking that way is that once you stop creating and posting videos your audience will leave your site. Once they are gone for good you can goodbye to your income.

Keep your audience updated and informed. Post updates in video form often and when you cannot create videos either post quick text explanations or find a source of alternative content. When you have to go away for an extended period of time because of a vacation, illness, or other event let your viewers know why you will be absent and for how long you will be absent. This will let them know that you are not one of the many vloggers out there who suddenly disappear without a word.

If you can try to find someone to manage your video blog for you while you are away. A guest video blogger can create some content in your place for awhile or even manage the upload of your alternative content. If you fail to do this then do not be surprised to come back from your absence to find that you now have an extremely small reader list.

Now that you know what video blogs are, how to build them, and how to drive traffic to them you are ready to start your own profitable video blog. If you utilize all of the resources referenced in this ebook you will have no trouble turning your video blog into a popular source of steady income. Even though this ebook contains the most current promotional technique and resources always be on the look out for something new since companies are coming up with new ways to reach video bloggers each and every day.

Printed by Libri Plureos GmbH in Hamburg,
Germany